Stanko Radmilovic

Current and developing trends in 2000-11 (55 countries, 11 indicators)

GRIN Verlag

Bibliografische Information der Deutschen Nationalbibliothek:

Die Deutsche Bibliothek verzeichnet diese Publikation in der Deutschen National-
bibliografie; detaillierte bibliografische Daten sind im Internet über http://dnb.d-
nb.de/ abrufbar.

Imprint:

Copyright © 2013 GRIN Verlag GmbH
Druck und Bindung: Books on Demand GmbH, Norderstedt Germany
ISBN: 978-3-656-59248-8

This book at GRIN:

http://www.grin.com/en/e-book/267569/current-and-developing-trends-in-2000-11-
55-countries-11-indicators

Prof. dr Stanko Radmilovic

M1. INDICATORS (11) ON CURRENT AND DEVELOPING TRENDS IN 2000-11 IN 55 COUNTRIES

Introductory accents

With the rates of economic growth we have dealt with recently in an article Paradox - the illusion of faster growth of GDP per capita in US$ than real economic growth - Comparative analysis for 69 countries, but with different pretensions:

1) to identify which countries, groups, the most vulnerable to the impact of the global economic crisis, and

2) to fully unmask the paradox that GDP per capita in current U.S. $, grows almost independently of the movement of rates of growth, but much more: (a) from depreciation U.S. $ as the de facto world of money, and (b) from unrealistic exchange rate parity.

In the article Economic movements (growth rate) 2000-12, in 55 countries ranked and segmented, our goal is different, more fundamental - and indicators contained in this article shall facilitate the achievement of this goal -:

1) once again (as we deal with this issue in many of the articles on this site www.radmilovicstanko.com) emphasize the enormous and far-reaching dedabalanse in economic growth rates between key countries and groups in the world, and

2) to discover / clarify as much as possible causes / factors on which it depends.

I am aware that the question of the imbalance in economic growth rates are quite different views and reviews, which are reduced approximately to:

(i) it is a well-known effect of low statistical base;

(ii) or, less statistical jargon, this is a elemenarnoj logic that is easier to achieve high growth rate at low levels of development, and vice versa.

That is true, but not the whole truth.

The table below shows that many countries with the same or similar baseline characteristics (as seen in many articles on this site, and otherwise, that are generally known facts) result in significantly different current and development results.

In order to obtain the desired information / answers, obviously require a wider and more versatile analigtička research. And this can not be achieved by looking investment and savings (accumulation), which we presented in the article M2. Interaction between of economic growth, investment and savings (accumulation) - comparative analysis of the pre-crisis and crisis period, for 69 countries. And we did it just because many consider primarily the size of savings and investment (despite achieving more than weak domestic savings accumulation) is key to boosting economic development. But it is obvious that with only two or three, and several indicators, we do not know and discover much more.

Therefore, I am now prepared a much larger set of indicators (11 in 55 countries and 12 years) for much more complex research analysis, and conceptualization the strategy for the recovery and development. That set publish this article and place it at the disposal of economic analysts and researchers. Of course I'll contribute. in this sense, of course, commensurate with my abilities.

Indicators for the analysis of current and developing trends in the period 2000-11

Ranking and segmentation were carried out on the basis of the average of 2000-11

The explanation of the categories is at the foot of the table

	Count.	GDP growth (ann. %)	Agricul., value added (% of GDP)	Indust., value added (% of GDP)	Servic., etc., value added (% of GDP)	Gen. Gover. final consum. expend. (ann. % growth)	Househ. final consum. expen., etc. (% of GDP)	Gross capital format. (% of GDP)	Extern. balance on goods and servic. (% of GDP)	Capit. coeff. (I 2000-10)/ (GDP 2001-11)	Gross domes. savings (in % of GDP)	FDI, net inflows (in % of GDP)
1	2	3	4	5	6	7	8	9	10	11	12	13
Countries with very high averages of growth rates												
1	Qatar	13,1					15,6	33,5	30,6	1,6	64,1	3,8
2	China	10,2	12,0	46,5	41,5	9,3	38,8	42,5	4,5	2,2	47,0	3,6
3	India	7,2	19,4	27,3	53,3	5,9	59,5	32,2	-3,0	2,3	29,1	1,6
Countries with high averages of growth rates												
4	Belar.	7,1	10,5	41,1	48,5	0,9	55,4	31,0	-5,4	2,7	25,6	2,4
5	Indone.	5,3	14,6	46,3	39,1	7,6	60,7	26,3	4,8	1,4	31,1	0,7
6	Russ.	5,3	5,2	35,8	59,0	1,5	49,4	21,7	11,3	1,3	33,0	2,5
7	Alban.	5,2	22,7	19,1	58,2	5,3	87,9	26,2	-23,3	2,6	2,9	6,1
8	Mold.	5,1	18,3	17,7	64,0	7,0	91,6	27,3	-37,2	1,8	-9,9	6,2
Countries with medium-high averages of growth rates												
9	UAEmir.	4,9	1,5	52,9	45,6	5,7	60,8	21,7	10,0	1,6	31,7	3,6
10	Eston.	4,7	3,7	28,4	67,9	2,5	54,8	29,9	-3,5	2,7	26,5	9,9
11	Lithuan.	4,6	4,6	30,9	64,5	3,0	64,9	21,5	-6,4	2,0	15,1	3,6
12	Ukra.	4,7	11,1	34,0	55,0	1,7	59,4	22,1	-0,4	1,7	21,7	4,3
13	Turk.	4,6	10,1	28,5	61,5	3,9	70,6	19,5	-2,9	1,6	16,6	1,7
14	Argen.	4,5	8,9	32,3	58,8		61,9	19,5	5,3	2,8	24,9	2,2
15	Korea	4,5	3,4	37,4	59,2	4,2	54,3	29,5	2,1	3,8	31,6	0,6
16	Latvia	4,4	4,0	22,4	73,6	-0,2	62,6	29,4	-10,9	2,8	18,5	4,3
17	Slovak	4,4	4,2	36,3	59,5	3,8	57,6	26,1	-2,9	2,5	23,2	4,7
18	Bulgar.	4,1	8,3	29,3	62,3	2,1	67,1	25,7	-10,6	2,3	15,1	12,3
19	Poland	4,0	4,4	30,8	64,8	3,9	63,4	21,2	-2,4	2,2	18,5	3,9
20	B - H	4,0	9,4	25,5	65,0		91,4	21,8	-37,3	2,2	-15,4	4,6
21	Rom.	3,9	10,5	37,1	52,4	7,0	71,2	24,5	-8,0	1,9	16,5	4,6
22	Israel	3,8				2,1	56,8	18,1	-0,5	2,4	17,6	4,1
23	Sa. Arab.	3,7	3,4	54,3	34,0	8,6	32,4	20,4	23,7	1,7	44,1	3,4
24	Serbia	3,7	12,8	28,4	58,7	6,8	79,1	21,1	-20,3	1,8	0,8	3,9
25	Brazil	3,6	6,0	28,0	66,1	2,9	61,0	17,9	1,0	1,1	18,9	2,9
26	Monten.	3,6	10,6	21,7	67,7		79,2	23,6	-27,2	2,2	-3,6	
27	Venezu.	3,5	4,5	51,9	43,6	6,4	52,9	24,0	10,8	2,6	34,8	1,3
28	So. Afric.	3,5	3,1	31,6	65,3	4,6	61,8	18,5	0,2	1,5	18,6	1,7
Countries with medium-low averages of growth rates												
29	Czech	3,4	2,9	36,1	61,1	1,6	50,3	27,3	1,4	2,5	28,8	5,3

30	Australia	3,0	3,1	24,3	72,6	2,9	56,8	26,6	-1,0	1,9	25,7	3,2
31	Ireland	2,9	1,9	36,2	61,9	2,9	47,0	21,4	14,4	3,7	35,8	15,0
32	Maced.	2,8	11,8	29,5	58,7	1,1	76,2	23,0	-18,7	2,2	4,3	5,4
33	Cyprus	2,8	3,0	19,2	77,8	3,3	65,7	19,5	-3,4	2,3	14,8	7,4
34	Sloven.	2,7	2,7	34,1	63,2	3,1	55,1	26,3	-0,6	3,4	25,7	2,3
35	Swed.	2,5	1,8	27,5	70,7	1,0	48,2	18,4	7,0	2,2	25,4	4,7
36	Croat.	2,5	5,5	27,9	66,7	1,2	59,4	25,3	-5,1	3,0	20,3	5,2
37	Mexico	2,4	3,9	33,0	63,2	1,1	66,3	24,0	-1,7	3,8	22,4	2,8
38	Can.	2,2	2,0	31,9	66,1	2,8	56,3	21,4	2,4	2,4	23,8	3,5
39	Finl.	2,2	3,0	32,4	64,7	1,2	51,9	20,5	5,1	2,9	25,6	3,6
40	Hung.	2,2	4,4	30,4	65,2	1,2	55,5	23,1	0,3	2,6	23,3	11,5
41	Spain	2,2	3,4	28,6	68,0	4,3	58,0	27,0	-3,6	3,5	23,4	3,8
Countries with low average growth rates												
42	Switz.	1,9		26,3		1,0	59,0	21,6	8,1	2,2	29,7	5,0
43	U.K.	1,9	0,8	23,7	75,4	2,1	64,5	16,7	-2,3	3,6	14,4	5,0
44	U.S.	1,8	1,2	21,7	77,2	2,0	70,3	18,0	-4,4	4,7	13,6	1,7
45	Austria	1,8	1,8	29,6	68,7	1,2	54,5	22,8	4,0	3,0	26,8	5,0
46	Norw.	1,7	1,6	40,9	57,6	2,4	43,0	21,6	14,6	2,2	36,3	3,0
47	Belg.	1,6	1,0	24,2	74,9	1,7	52,3	21,4	3,4	2,9	24,8	16,4
48	Netherl.	1,6	2,2	24,4	73,4	2,9	47,8	19,7	7,4	2,9	27,0	6,0
49	Greece	1,5				2,1	70,6	22,9	-11,9	3,4	11,0	0,8
50	France	1,4	2,4	21,1	76,5	1,6	57,0	19,9	-0,6	2,9	19,3	2,7
51	Germ.	1,3	1,0	29,3	69,7	1,2	57,9	18,5	4,6	2,9	23,2	2,0
52	Denm.	0,9	1,7	25,0	73,3	1,5	48,2	20,2	4,8	3,0	25,0	3,3
53	Japan	0,8	1,3	28,4	70,3	1,9	58,1	22,3	1,0	6,0	23,3	0,2
54	Portu.	0,7	2,9	25,3	71,8	1,5	64,7	23,3	-8,3	3,7	15,0	3,5
55	Italy	0,7	2,3	26,9	70,8	1,4	59,5	20,8	-0,1	3,4	20,7	1,1

Data source for making / processing of these indicators: WB DataBank, maj 2013

The explanation of the categories in col. 3-13:

GDP growth (annual %) (Col. 3): Annual percentage growth rate of GDP at market prices based on constant local currency. Aggregates are based on constant 2000 U.S. dollars. GDP is the sum of gross value added by all resident producers in the economy plus any product taxes and minus any subsidies not included in the value of the products. It is calculated without making deductions for depreciation of fabricated assets or for depletion and degradation of natural resources.

Agriculture, value added (% of GDP) (Col. 4): Agriculture corresponds to ISIC divisions 1-5 and includes forestry, hunting, and fishing, as well as cultivation of crops and livestock production. Value added is the net output of a sector after adding up all outputs and subtracting intermediate inputs. It is calculated without making deductions for depreciation of fabricated assets or depletion and degradation of natural resources. The origin of value added is determined by the International Standard Industrial Classification (ISIC), revision 3. Note: For VAB countries, gross value added at factor cost is used as the denominator.

Industry, value added (% of GDP) (Col. 5): Industry corresponds to ISIC divisions 10-45 and includes manufacturing (ISIC divisions 15-37). It comprises value added in mining, manufacturing (also reported as a separate subgroup), construction, electricity, water, and gas. Value added is the net output of a sector after adding up all outputs and subtracting intermediate inputs. It is calculated without making deductions for depreciation of fabricated assets or depletion and degradation of natural resources. The origin of value added is determined by the International Standard Industrial Classification (ISIC), revision 3. Note: For VAB countries, gross value added at factor cost is used as the denominator.

Services, etc., value added (% of GDP) (Col. 6): Services correspond to ISIC divisions 50-99 and they include value added in wholesale and retail trade (including hotels and restaurants), transport, and government, financial, professional, and personal services such as education, health care, and real estate services. Also included are imputed bank service charges, import duties, and any statistical discrepancies noted by national compilers as well as discrepancies arising from rescaling. Value added is the net output of a sector after adding up all outputs and subtracting intermediate inputs. It is calculated without making deductions for depreciation of fabricated assets or depletion and degradation of natural resources. The industrial origin of value added is determined by the International Standard Industrial Classification (ISIC), revision 3. Note: For VAB countries, gross value added at factor cost is used as the denominator.

General government final consumption expenditure (annual % growth) (Col. 7): Annual percentage growth of general government final consumption expenditure based on constant local currency. Aggregates are based on constant 2000 U.S. dollars. General government final consumption expenditure (general government consumption) includes all government current expenditures for purchases of goods and services (including compensation of employees). It also includes most expenditures on national defense and security, but excludes government military expenditures that are part of government capital formation.

Household final consumption expenditure, etc. (% of GDP) (Col. 8): Household final consumption expenditure (formerly private consumption) is the market value of all goods and services, including durable products (such as cars, washing machines, and home computers), purchased by households. It excludes purchases of dwellings but includes imputed rent for owner-occupied dwellings. It also includes payments and fees to governments to obtain permits and licenses. Here, household consumption expenditure includes the expenditures of nonprofit institutions serving households, even when reported separately by the country. This item also includes any statistical discrepancy in the use of resources relative to the supply of resources.

Gross capital formation (% of GDP) (Col. 9): Gross capital formation (formerly gross domestic investment) consists of outlays on additions to the fixed assets of the economy plus net changes in the level of inventories. Fixed assets include land improvements (fences, ditches, drains, and so on); plant, machinery, and equipment purchases; and the construction of roads, railways, and the like, including schools, offices, hospitals, private residential dwellings, and commercial and industrial buildings. Inventories are stocks of goods held by firms to meet temporary or unexpected fluctuations in production or sales, and "work in progress." According to the 1993 SNA, net acquisitions of valuables are also considered capital formation.

External balance on goods and services (% of GDP) (Col. 10): External balance on goods and services (formerly resource balance) equals exports of goods and services minus imports of goods and services (previously nonfactor services).

CAPITAL COEFFICIENT (col. 11): the ratio of the value of capital (ΔI) to the value of output (ΔGDP)

Gross domestic savings (% of GDP) (Col. 12): Gross domestic savings are calculated as GDP less final consumption expenditure (total consumption).

Foreign direct investment, net inflows (% of GDP) (Col. 13): Foreign direct investment are the net inflows of investment to acquire a lasting management interest (10 percent or more of voting stock) in an enterprise operating in an economy other than that of the investor. It is the sum of equity capital, reinvestment of earnings, other long-term capital, and short-term capital as shown in the balance of payments. This series shows net inflows (new investment inflows less disinvestment) in the reporting economy from foreign investors, and is divided by GDP.